The S...
CA...
JANE

Bruce T.
Paddock

Boston, Massachusetts
Chandler, Arizona
Glenview, Illinois
Upper Saddle River, New Jersey

Illustrations
5, 9, 10, 11, 14, 15 Tim Jones; 7 Joe LeMonnier.

Photographs
Every effort has been made to secure permission and provide appropriate credit for photographic material.
The publisher deeply regrets any omission and pledges to correct errors called to its attention in subsequent editions.

Unless otherwise acknowledged, all photographs are the property of Pearson Education, Inc.

Photo locators denoted as follows: Top (T), Center (C), Bottom (B), Left (L), Right (R), Background (Bkgd)

Opener: Prints & Photographs Division, LC-USZ62-47390/Library of Congress; 1 Prints & Photographs Division,
LC-USZ62-47390/Library of Congress; 2 Prints & Photographs Division, LC-USZ62-50004/Library of Congress; 4 Prints &
Photographs Division, LC-USZ62-75148/Library of Congress; 6 National Archives, Pacific Region; 8 Prints & Photographs
Division, LC-DIG-ppmsca-13514/Library of Congress; 12 Prints & Photographs Division, LC-USZ62-47390/Library of
Congress; 13 Prints & Photographs Division, LC-USZ62-47389/Library of Congress.

Copyright © 2013 by Pearson Education, Inc., or its affiliates. All rights
reserved. Printed in the United States of America. This publication is protected
by copyright, and permission should be obtained from the publisher prior to
any prohibited reproduction, storage in a retrieval system, or transmission in
any form by any means, electronic, mechanical, photocopying, recording, or
likewise. For information regarding permissions, write to Pearson Curriculum
Rights & Permissions, One Lake Street, Upper Saddle River, New Jersey 07458.

Pearson® is a trademark, in the U.S. and/or in other countries,
of Pearson Inc. or its affiliates.

ISBN-13: 978-0-328-67709-2
ISBN-10:   0-328-67709-4

7 8 9 10 V0SI 18 17 16 15

The Old West

After the Civil War ended in 1865, many Americans moved west of the Mississippi River. Some looked for quiet and **solitude** beyond the crowded Eastern cities. Others saw an opportunity to make a better life. And a few others sought to **reinvent** themselves in the West. Some wanted to be free of their past.

Martha Jane Cannary was one person who reinvented herself in the Old West. Like many children, she moved west with her family. When Martha Cannary was still a teenager, her parents died and she was left on her own. Eventually she gave herself a new name, Calamity Jane, and reinvented herself.

If Calamity felt that her life wasn't exciting enough, she made up wild stories about herself. Soon other people were making up stories about her as well. As a result of all this storytelling, it's hard to know for sure who the real Calamity Jane was.

Meet Calamity Jane

Martha Jane Cannary said she was born on May 1, 1852. She likely changed her true birth date. For her, part of the excitement of moving west was changing her past.

Her Early Life

From what historians can tell, the Cannary family was quite poor. They lived in a simple cabin on a small farm outside of Princeton, Missouri. Sometime in 1865, the family left Missouri and moved to Virginia City, Montana.

By this time, Martha Cannary had two younger brothers and three younger sisters. During the trip west, she probably spent as much time on horseback, riding with the men and hunting, as she did sitting in the wagons with the other children.

Looking back at this time, she said, "I was at all times with the men when there was excitement and adventure to be had . . . . I was considered a remarkable good shot and a fearless rider for a girl my age." It is probably true that she was a good rider and shooter.

Martha's mother died in early 1866. Shortly after that, the family moved to Utah, but just about a year later, her father died.

After the Civil War people traveled west by railroad and wagon train.

"Calamity Jane" Is Born

No one knows for sure what happened after Martha's parents died. Some say that she and her siblings may have moved to Wyoming. Others say her brothers and sisters were sent to Salt Lake City, Utah.

At this time, American **society** had strict rules about how a young woman such as Martha was supposed to act. A typical young woman lived with her parents until she got married. After that, she was expected to obey her husband.

It's clear that Martha Cannary wanted no part of such a life. The wide-open land and attitudes in the West let her break free of society's rules. The fact that she had no parents also played a role.

In the late 1860s or early 1870s, Martha began roaming across the West. Her **reputation** spread as an excellent rider and a crack, or first-rate, shot. In 1876 she arrived in Deadwood, South Dakota. She was no longer Martha Cannary, but a rough-living, tough-talking woman who called herself Calamity Jane. A calamity is something that causes trouble.

Calamity Jane
in her early twenties

The Deadwood Years

In the early 1870s, gold was discovered in the Black Hills of South Dakota. The United States government tried to keep this news quiet because the land belonged to the Lakota Native Americans. However, the news eventually got out and a **gold rush** followed.

Wild Bill Hickok was a celebrity, known throughout the country for his famous deeds.

Prospectors found gold in a narrow canyon called Deadwood Gulch. In 1876, the town of Deadwood grew up in that gulch. Deadwood started as a crude mining camp with people living in tents or in shacks of scrap wood.

Wild Bill Hickok

When Calamity Jane arrived in Deadwood, the town had no laws and no sheriff. Calamity fit right in. So did another famous figure of the Old West called Wild Bill Hickok. He moved to Deadwood at about the same time as Calamity Jane.

When Hickok arrived in Deadwood, he was already a famous Army scout, lawman, and gunfighter. Calamity admired him, as many people did. It seems, though, that they were only neighbors for a few weeks. Hickok was murdered soon after he settled in Deadwood.

Deadwood was barely a town when Calamity arrived, but it grew up quickly.

Good Deeds in Deadwood

Gradually, Deadwood started to become a quieter and less wild town. A sheriff arrived in 1876. Shopkeepers began to move in, and bandits began to move out.

It's possible that life in Deadwood was now getting too dull for Calamity. She may have spent some of this time as a rider carrying mail sacks back and forth between Deadwood and Custer City. She later said that this trail "was considered the most dangerous route" in the Black Hills. However, since her "reputation as a rider and quick shot was well known," bandits left her alone.

Then, in 1878, smallpox swept through the Black Hills. Calamity bravely took care of her friends and neighbors who were stricken with the deadly disease. Some people said that this was not the only time in her life when she acted as an unpaid, untrained nurse. They say she often looked after people suffering from illness.

Time Away from Deadwood

In 1879, Calamity took a job as a bullwhacker. Back then, freight wagons were usually pulled by bulls or oxen, not horses. Bullwhackers drove the wagons from one dusty town to another, cracking whips over the animal's heads to keep them moving.

Once she was on the road again, Calamity just kept moving. She said she spent several years driving wagon trains and freight wagons. At some point before 1891, she may have met and married a man named Clinton Burk. They may also have raised a daughter. But no one knows for sure if this was true.

According to Calamity, she and Burk moved to Boulder, Colorado, and opened a hotel. Perhaps they did. She also says they wandered through Wyoming, Montana, Idaho, Washington, and Oregon. It's unlikely we'll ever know for sure. But it does seem true that she never stayed in one place too long.

Calamity Jane claimed to have been in many places in the Old West.

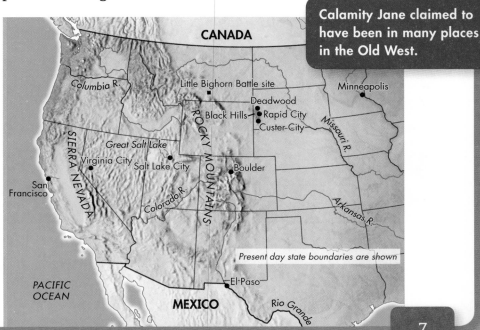

Return to Deadwood

In 1895, Calamity arrived back in Deadwood with a daughter. The girl was sent to a private school. What happened to this girl? Maybe she died young. Maybe she grew up and lived a normal life. We don't know for sure.

By this time, the Old West was disappearing, and people were already **nostalgic** for it. All across the United States, people wanted to experience the "Wild West," even if they had never been there. Buffalo Bill Cody was touring the United States and Europe with his "Wild West" show. Calamity thought she could make money this way, too. She appeared in shows at the Palace Museum in Minneapolis, Minnesota, in 1896 and at a world's fair, the Pan-American Exposition, in Buffalo, New York, in 1901.

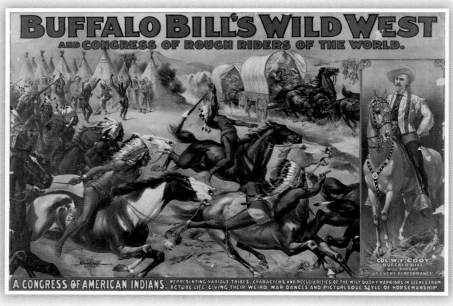

People loved seeing shows that they thought represented the old "Wild West."

This illustration is based on a photo taken near the end of Calamity's life.

Calamity Jane's Last Days

Although Calamity considered Deadwood her home, she still kept wandering. On August 1, 1903, she was on a train headed out of Deadwood when she became ill. After the train stopped in Terry, South Dakota, Calamity got off and rented a room in a shabby hotel where she died that night. She was buried in Deadwood next to Wild Bill Hickok's grave.

After Calamity's death, Buffalo Bill is reported to have said, "Only the old days could have produced her. She belongs to a time and a class that are fast disappearing."

He was probably right. Without the freedom—and even the lawlessness—of the Old West, Martha Cannary could never have become Calamity Jane.

It is hard to separate truth from fiction in Calamity Jane's life.

A Closer Look at Calamity Jane's Life

Thanks to the freedom of the West—and her own strong personality—Calamity Jane seems to have led the life she wanted to live. Yet, when we examine Calamity Jane's life, we find that it's very difficult to figure out what was true and what was fiction.

For example, her actual birth date is uncertain. In a short autobiography, Calamity said she was born on May 1, 1852. If that were so, she would have been 51 when she died. However, her original gravestone said she died at age 53. She may never have known her own real birth date.

There are other questions about her life. Let's take a closer look to see if we can determine what's true and what's not.

Did Calamity Jane Serve in the Army?

In her autobiography, Calamity said she spent the time from 1870 to 1876 as an Army scout. She claimed that she served under General George Custer, among others. Of this time, she wrote:

"I had a great many adventures . . . for as a scout I had a great many dangerous missions to perform and while I was in many close places always succeeded in getting away safely for by this time I was considered the most reckless and daring rider and one of the best shots in the western country."

Calamity claimed that in 1876 she was **dispatched** to carry messages to General Custer. She said she swam across a river and then rode until she became ill. She was ordered to stop and rest. Had that not happened, she wrote, she would have been with Custer at the Battle of the Little Big Horn, in which Native Americans defeated Custer and killed most of his men.

This is an interesting story, but it probably never happened. Calamity probably did work as a bullwhacker. She may also have been an unofficial scout or messenger for an Army company. But there's no evidence that she was ever on the Army payroll—or met General Custer.

Calamity Jane was buried near Deadwood, South Dakota.

Where Did Calamity Jane Get Her Name?

Calamity claimed she got her nickname in 1872 or 1873, in a battle with Native Americans. When she saw a wounded captain about to fall off his horse, she raced over, grabbed him, and whisked him away to safety. After the captain recovered, he said, "I name you Calamity Jane, **heroine** of the plains." Again, it's an exciting story, but historians generally agree that this event never took place.

So where did the nickname, Calamity Jane, come from then? Women in the Old West were often called "Jane." Maybe Martha was called Calamity Jane because she was a woman and a calamity—or trouble—always seemed to follow her. Maybe she was such a troublemaker that her arrival was seen as a calamity. There are lots of possibilities. In the end, though, we'll never know how she got her famous nickname.

This photo was probably taken during the brief time Calamity appeared at the Pan-American Exposition in Buffalo, New York, in 1901.

Calamity posed for this picture in front of her "good friend" Wild Bill Hickok's grave sometime in the 1880s.

Was She Friends with Wild Bill Hickok?

In her later years, Calamity often said that Wild Bill Hickok was "my good friend." She said that when she heard of his death, she rushed out of her room and tracked down Bill's murderer. She said she cornered him until the sheriff arrived to arrest him. This event never happened.

Toward the end of her life, Calamity claimed that she and Hickok had been secretly married. They were never married, since Hickok was married to someone else during the time he was in Deadwood. It's clear, though, that Calamity strongly admired Hickok, even twenty-five years after his death. It was her request that she be buried next to him.

Did Calamity Jane Get Married?

Calamity said that when she left Deadwood around 1879, she joined the U.S. Cavalry. If she did, there's no record of it. She also said she traveled to San Francisco, Arizona, and Texas, but there's no evidence of this, either. While in Texas, she wrote,

"I met Mr. Clinton Burk, a native of Texas, who I married in August 1885. As I thought I had traveled through life long enough alone and thought it was about time to take a partner for the rest of my days."

Burk may have been from El Paso, but Calamity most likely never visited there. While she may have hoped that her marriage would last, it was not to be. By the time she returned to Deadwood, she and Burk had split up.

Was Calamity Jane a "Wild West" Star?

Many people think that Calamity spent the last years of her life starring in "Wild West" shows. But all we know for sure is that she was in one show in Minneapolis in 1896 and one in Buffalo in 1901. Did she star in other shows? Maybe she did. Or maybe she decided she didn't like speaking in front of crowds. Some sources say she got fired from the only two shows she ever was hired to do.

So Who Was Calamity Jane?

Calamity Jane was a great storyteller, and she did a great job of reinventing herself. As a result, historians have trouble telling fact from fiction about her life. Yet, one writer who helped create the **legend** of Calamity Jane never claimed to have written anything other than fiction.

Wheeler's books added to the legend of Calamity Jane.

Ned Wheeler was a writer in the East. He wrote western stories, even though he'd never been west of Pennsylvania. In 1877, Wheeler started writing stories about a fictional cowboy named Deadwood Dick. Later, Wheeler decided he needed to give Dick a rough-riding, straight-shooting costar. He named this character Calamity Jane.

Wheeler described his Calamity Jane as brave and beautiful. She had more adventures than even the real Calamity Jane claimed to have had. More than once, Wheeler's Calamity Jane came riding in to save Deadwood Dick from certain death.

Wheeler may have known about the real Calamity Jane. He never said. But there was a real Calamity Jane. And she devoted her life to creating her own stories about herself. The true story of Calamity Jane, star of the Old West, is hard to know. But her legend lives on.

Glossary

dispatch to send someone on a mission

gold rush the quick movement of many people to a place after gold is discovered there

heroine a female hero

legend a story, or group of stories, that many people believe but that cannot be proven to be true

nostalgic longing for something in the past

reinvent to change completely into something new

reputation what people think about a person

society people as a group, who share a system of laws and beliefs

solitude being alone or far away from others